THE SCIENCE BEHIND
BATMAN'S
UNIFORM

DC COMICS™
SUPER HEROES

by
Agnieszka Biskup

BATMAN created by
Bob Kane with Bill Finger

SCIENCE BEHIND
BATMAN

Curious Fox
a capstone company-publishers for children

Published by Curious Fox, an imprint of Capstone Global Library Limited, 7 Pilgrim Street, London, EC4V 6LB –
Registered company number: 6695582

www.curious-fox.com

STAR37305

ISBN 978 1 78202 541 2
20 19 18 17 16
10 9 8 7 6 5 4 3 2 1

British Library Cataloguing in Publication Data
A full catalogue record for this book is available from the British Library.

Editorial Credits
Christopher Harbo, editor; Hilary Wacholz, designer; Wanda Winch, media researcher;
Tori Abraham, production specialist

Artwork by Luciano Vecchio and Ethen Beavers

Photo Credits
Alamy: Jeff Mood, 9 (right); Dreamstime: Lawrence Weslowski Jr., 13 (left); Getty Images: Denver Post/Ernie
Leyba, 15 (l); Glow Images: Science Faction/SuperStock, 13 (r); NASA, 7 (bottom left); Newscom: ZUMA Press/
ChinaFotoPress, 20; Shutterstock: TFoxFoto, 9 (l), Fotokostic, 10, 501room, 10 (inset), Alexandra Lande, 19; U.S.
Navy: PH2 John L. Beeman, 7 (top right), MC3 Billy Ho, 16, Lt. Troy Wilcox, 17; Wikimedia: J. Glover, Atlanta,
Georgia, 15 (r)

Printed in China.

CONTENTS

INTRODUCTION
BEHIND THE BATSUIT

Most super heroes have incredible powers. But not Batman. He fights crime with science and engineering. His Batsuit is loaded with amazing **technology**. Best of all, the science behind his suit is found in our world too.

technology use of science to do practical things such as designing complex machines

Batman's suit protects him from deadly impacts.

Batman's mask protects his head and hides his identity.

Batman's Utility Belt contains many gadgets and weapons.

Batman's cape allows him to glide through the air.

Batman's suit keeps him warm and protects against fiery explosions.

CHAPTER 1

BATMAN'S BODYSUIT

Batman's **bodysuit** keeps him warm during cold nights. In our world, **neoprene** bodysuits help divers to stay warm. The rubber-like material contains tiny bubbles of gas. These bubbles help to stop heat from leaving a diver's body.

This diver is wearing a neoprene wetsuit to stay warm in the water.

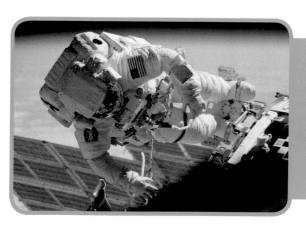

FACT

Spacesuits have layers that protect astronauts from heat, cold and flying objects.

bodysuit close-fitting one-piece article of clothing, typically worn for sport
neoprene strong, waterproof material sometimes used to make wetsuits

Batman's suit protects him from fiery explosions.

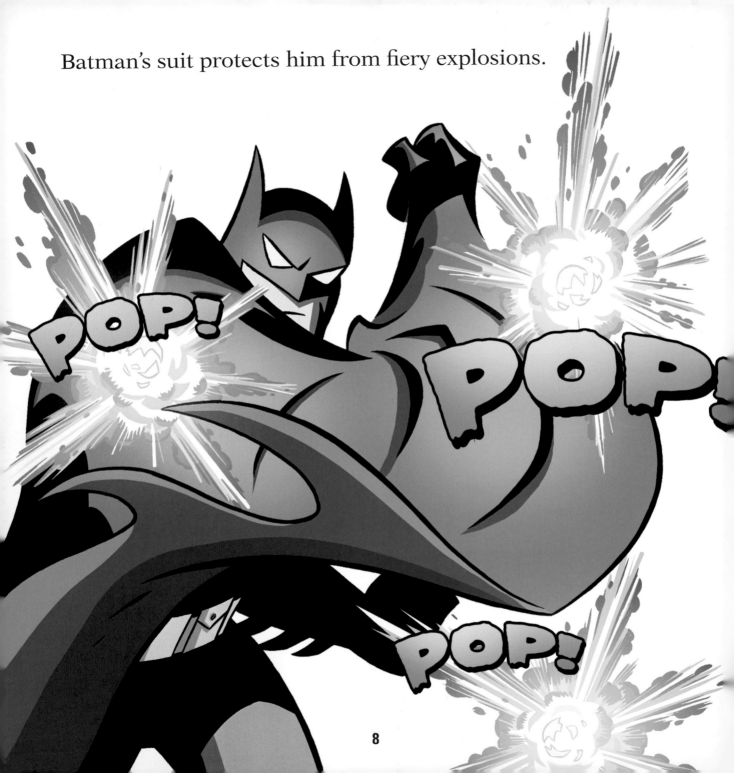

Nomex in a firefighter's uniform protects against the heat of a fire.

In the real world, clothing made from Nomex protects racing car drivers and firefighters against burns. This material has special **fibres** that thicken when fire touches them. The swelling fibres protect the skin from heat.

FACT

Stunt people wear Nomex suits to film fiery scenes in films.

fibre long, thin thread of material

The Batsuit helps to shield the Caped Crusader from deadly **impacts**. In our world, police officers wear bulletproof vests made from Kevlar. This fabric gets its strength from tightly woven fibres.

Inside police vests are many layers of tightly woven Kevlar.

impact striking of one thing against another
ceramic made of materials that are hardened by heat

FACT

Some body armour has **ceramic** plates. These plates are as strong as steel, but are much lighter.

11

CHAPTER 2
THE CAPED CRUSADER'S COWL

Batman's **cowl** hides his face and protects his head. In real life, soldiers and athletes protect their heads with helmets. Their helmets have hard shells and soft foam linings. A hard shell spreads the force of an impact over a large area. A foam lining **absorbs** the energy of the impact.

Pit crew members wear helmets to protect against accidents during races.

Military helmets often include Kevlar to protect against bullets.

cowl hood or long hooded cloak

absorb soak up

The ears of Batman's cowl carry microphones for spying on villains. In our world, **parabolic** microphones help with long-distance listening. These bowl-shaped devices can record sounds up to 270 metres (300 yards) away.

A parabolic microphone picks up sounds at a sporting event.

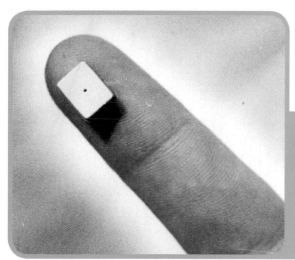

FACT

Bugs are hidden microphones that secretly pick up sounds. They can be as small as your fingertip.

parabolic shaped like a bowl

Night-vision lenses help Batman to see in the dark. Real night-vision equipment uses either **thermal** imaging or image **enhancement**. Thermal imaging lets you see heat given off by objects. Image enhancement boosts available light to make objects look brighter.

A soldier tests the settings on night-vision goggles.

FACT

Night-vision goggles with image enhancement show objects in green. Why? Because our eyes can see more shades of green than any other colour.

thermal relating to heat

enhancement making something clearer or larger

CHAPTER 3
THE DARK KNIGHT'S CAPE

Similar to a hang-glider, Batman's cape helps him to glide through the air. A hang-glider is a curved, triangle-shaped wing. It rises when air flows over its surface to create **lift**. Hang-glider pilots can easily soar 160 kilometres (100 miles) in a single flight.

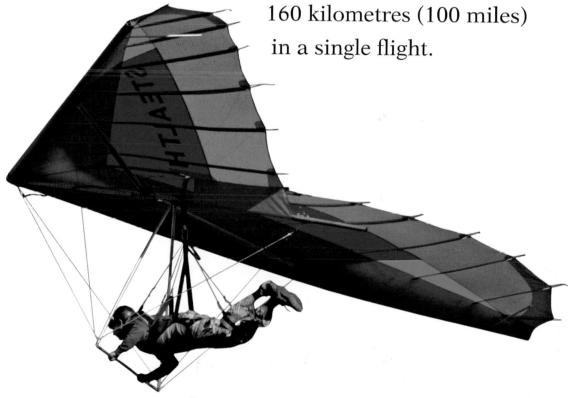

lift upward force of air that causes an object to fly

Some people use wingsuits to glide like Batman. These suits have webbing between the legs and under the arms. During a jump, air fills the webbing to help wingsuiters glide like flying squirrels. Wingsuiters then use parachutes to land safely.

A wingsuiter glides through the air above Tianmen Mountain in China.

The Batsuit seems like a simple
disguise, but it's really the ultimate
super hero body armour. The real
science behind it is as amazing as
the Caped Crusader it protects.

21

GLOSSARY

absorb soak up

bodysuit close-fitting one-piece article of clothing, typically worn for sport

ceramic made of materials that are hardened by heat

cowl hood or long hooded cloak

enhancement making something clearer or larger

fibre long, thin thread of material

impact striking of one thing against another

lift upward force of air that causes an object to fly

neoprene strong, waterproof material sometimes used to make wetsuits

parabolic shaped like a bowl

technology use of science to do practical things such as designing complex machines

thermal relating to heat

READ MORE

Diary of a Firefighter (Diary of a…), Angela Royston (Raintree, 2014)

Extreme Sports, Emily Bone (Usborne, 2014)

How to Draw Batman and His Friends and Foes (Drawing DC Super Heroes), Aaron Sautter (Raintree, 2015)

Special Forces (Heroic Jobs), Ellen Labrecque (Raintree, 2013)

Spying, Henry Brook (Usborne, 2013)

INDEX

READ THEM ALL!

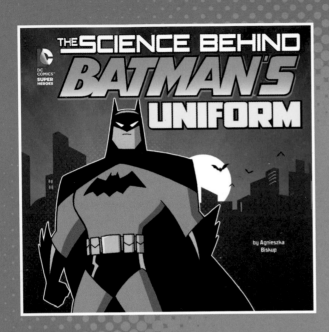

THE SCIENCE BEHIND
BATMAN'S UNIFORM
by Agnieszka Biskup

THE SCIENCE BEHIND
BATMAN'S GROUND VEHICLES
by Tammy Enz

THE SCIENCE BEHIND
BATMAN'S FLYING MACHINES
by Tammy Enz

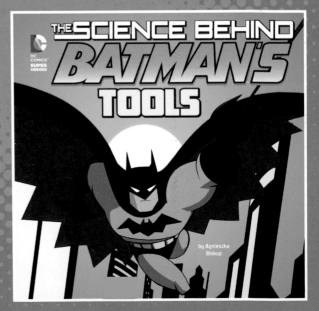

THE SCIENCE BEHIND
BATMAN'S TOOLS
by Agnieszka Biskup